SCIENTISTS IN THE FIELD

PALEONTOLOGISTS

Tom Greve

Rourke
Educational Media

rourkeeducationalmedia.com

Scan for Related Titles
and Teacher Resources

Before Reading:

Building Academic Vocabulary and Background Knowledge

Before reading a book, it is important to tap into what your child or students already know about the topic. This will help them develop their vocabulary, increase their reading comprehension, and make connections across the curriculum.

1. Look at the cover of the book. What will this book be about?
2. What do you already know about the topic?
3. Let's study the Table of Contents. What will you learn about in the book's chapters?
4. What would you like to learn about this topic? Do you think you might learn about it from this book? Why or why not?
5. Use a reading journal to write about your knowledge of this topic. Record what you already know about the topic and what you hope to learn about the topic.
6. Read the book.
7. In your reading journal, record what you learned about the topic and your response to the book.
8. After reading the book complete the activities below.

Content Area Vocabulary
Read the list. What do these words mean?

biology
catastrophic
chemistry
epochs
era
fossils
funding
half-life
Ice Age
physics
prehistoric
radioactivity
radiometric
sediment
specimen
strata

After Reading:

Comprehension and Extension Activity

After reading the book, work on the following questions with your child or students in order to check their level of reading comprehension and content mastery.

1. What is the difference between a trace fossil and a body fossil? (Summarize)
2. How has technology helped paleontologists? (Asking questions)
3. How can you contribute to research done by paleontologists? (Text to self connection)
4. How are paleontologists and archaeologists similar and different? (Summarize)
5. Why is it important to paleontologists to study fossils? (Asking questions)

Extension Activity

Paleontologists have helped us understand the prehistoric creatures that roamed the Earth millions of years ago. Research the dinosaur you find most interesting. Where was it found? What did it look like? What traits did it have to help it survive? Pretend you are a paleontologist who discovered the dinosaur you researched. Write an article for a scientific journal explaining your findings.

TABLE OF CONTENTS

IT'S ABOUT TIME

Kids always know how old they are. That is because they know their birthday, and it's easy to keep track by counting the years as they go by.

Knowing the age of our planet is not so simple. For one thing, the history of Earth is far longer than the history of human beings living on it.

FIELD NOTES

Scientists study rocks to learn how old the Earth might be. Human beings rarely live to be more than 100 years old. Though a century is a long time for a human to live, it is little more than a blink of an eye when considering the age of the planet itself.

Time is relative. To a kid, a year seems like a mighty long time to wait for a present or a vacation. But to the Earth, a year is like a split-second. Compared to an individual person, or even compared to the human race, Earth is unimaginably old.

The study of the Earth itself, what it is made of, and all that lies beneath the ground is the science of geology.

Geologists call the ground we walk on Earth's crust. Like a pie crust, Earth's outermost layer is a thin shell, which is even thinner under the ocean, and thicker where there is dry land.

HUMAN TIME vs GEOLOGICAL TIME

The late paleontologist Stephen J. Gould once said if a person's outstretched arms represented all of time since the Earth formed, the amount of time humans have witnessed could fit on the tip of a single fingernail. Not even the nail itself, just the tip of the nail. Everything else happened before humans were around to notice. In other words, nearly all of Earth's life is **prehistoric**.

So how do people know things about Earth from all that prehistoric time? Those answers come from a variety of sources, but many of the most astounding discoveries of prehistoric life on Earth come from paleontologists.

Paleontologists are like detectives trying to solve a case about the history of living things on this planet.

Fossils of some of Earth's earliest known humans, found by researchers at Atapuerca, a cave system in Spain, are relatively new fossils even though they are thought to be more than a half million years old.

FOSSILS AND THE MYSTERY OF PREHISTORY

The Earth buries its past. Imagine the bedroom floor of a messy kid getting buried deeper and deeper with clothes, toys, papers, and whatever he or she drops after coming home from school day after day. That is a bit like how Earth is littered with signs of life left behind over the course of millions and millions of years.

If a child never cleans their room, day after day, year after year, their stuff just piles up on the floor. Soon items are buried in the mess. If a hat or a baseball mitt gets dropped on the floor, finding that same hat or mitt months later would require digging into the mess to find it. This is the basic idea of paleontology: digging into the earth to find things that lived many years earlier.

DIGGING INTO THE PAST

Paleontologists and geologists call Earth's rock layers **strata**. Each layer represents time on Earth in the way the rings of a tree trunk mark the tree's age. If the messy kid wants to find a shirt she knows she left on the floor months ago, she'd have to dig down under more recent items she's dropped to find the old shirt. This is how a paleontologist finds evidence of once-living things from long ago. It's a matter of using science to know where to start looking, and figuring out which strata will likely hold what they're looking for.

Nature has a way of turning the remains of dead plants and animals from long ago into part of the buried rock layers.

Living things that die and then slowly become part of the Earth are called **fossils**. Fossilization is a process that turns plants and animals into imprints in Earth's rock layers. While a kid's toy ends up buried in a messy room after just days, a living thing takes millions of years, and some luck, in order to become a buried fossil.

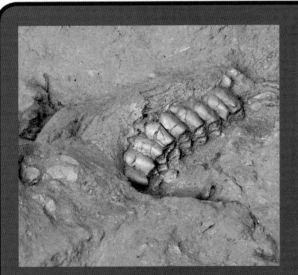

PALEONTOLOGY vs ARCHAEOLOGY

Though similar in many ways, paleontologists research, find, and study fossil remnants of all life forms, while archaeologists study human remains or artifacts.

Earth's crust is made of solid rocks and minerals. Its rocky layers are visible in many areas.

LOCATION, LOCATION, LOCATION

Most creatures die and never become fossils. For a fossil to form, animals need to die and have their remains become buried quickly before they decompose or get eaten by another animal. This happens best if the animal dies in a muddy, wet spot and their bones sink. The mud, or **sediment**, which covers up the skeleton, slowly turns to rock over millions of years.

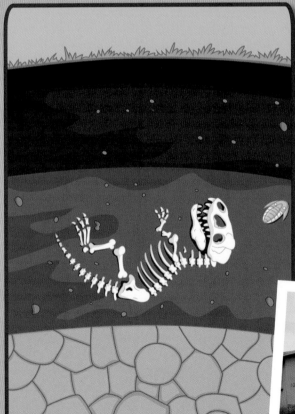

COUGHING UP FOSSILS
Sometimes **catastrophic** events such as earthquakes can lift buried sedimentary rock layers to the surface. Fossils that took millions of years to form might be thrust to the surface in a single quake.

MAKE FOSSILS

MINERAL REPLACEMENT

While the sediment holding the bones hardens, another chemical process slowly plays out again, over millions of years. Given enough time, minerals in the sediment will replace minerals in the bones. The process slowly turns the bones into a fossil.

FIELD NOTES

body fossil

trace fossil

A body fossil is one made by the remains of the actual animal. A trace fossil is something the animal left behind, such as a footprint.

A paleontologist's job is to find fossils and study them in order to make sense of what was going on here on Earth for billions of years before there were ever human beings.

Paleontologists have to take many science classes to become full-fledged fossil experts. Paleontology is a combination of several other areas of scientific study such as geology, **biology**, **chemistry**, and **physics**. If a young person really likes science, and finds the mystery of prehistory fascinating, then that person could be a budding paleontologist.

Once a fossil is found, great care and precision are needed to remove that fossil from surrounding rock. Here, a paleontologist carefully works on a fossilized bone of the dinosaur Europasaurus holgeri.

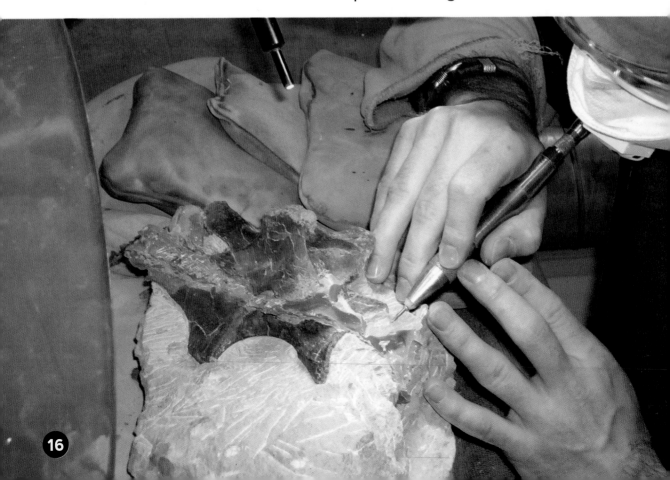

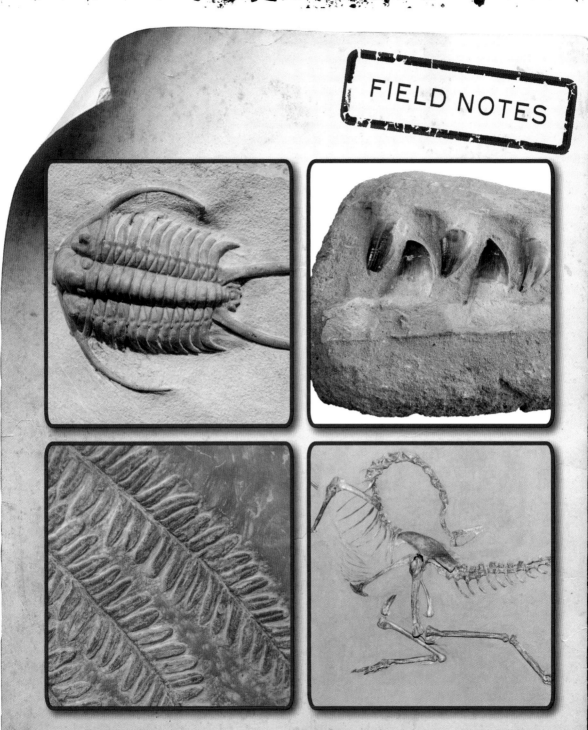

The scientific discovery and study of fossils, and their categorization based on time, species, location, and other factors, is known as the fossil record.

THE FOSSIL RECORD: SCIENTIFIC SCORECARD

The fossil record represents evidence of life here on planet Earth dating back millions, even billions of years. Much of the scientific knowledge about fossils however has happened courtesy of paleontologists over just the past few centuries.

SENSATIONAL SCIENTIST

Naturalist Charles Darwin studied living plants and animals before writing his theory of evolution through natural selection. His theory, that species change over time to better aid their chances at survival, seems to be on display in the fossil record. Although Darwin was not a paleontologist, his scientific work remains central to the science of paleontology today.

Charles Darwin
1809 -1882

Fossils of woolly mammoths, which looked similar but not identical to the skeletons of elephants, gave scientists like Cuvier a clear indication that the fossils were of an extinct species.

Paleontologists have a history of controversy because many of their scientific discoveries and contributions to the fossil record have differed over time from how most people, and many religions, perceive the Earth's past.

SENSATIONAL SCIENTIST

Many scientists call George Cuvier the father of paleontology. His study of fossils led him to the theory that some fossilized remains were of creatures that no longer existed on planet Earth. Cuvier's observation is the scientific community's first understanding of the idea of extinction.

George Cuvier
1769 -1832

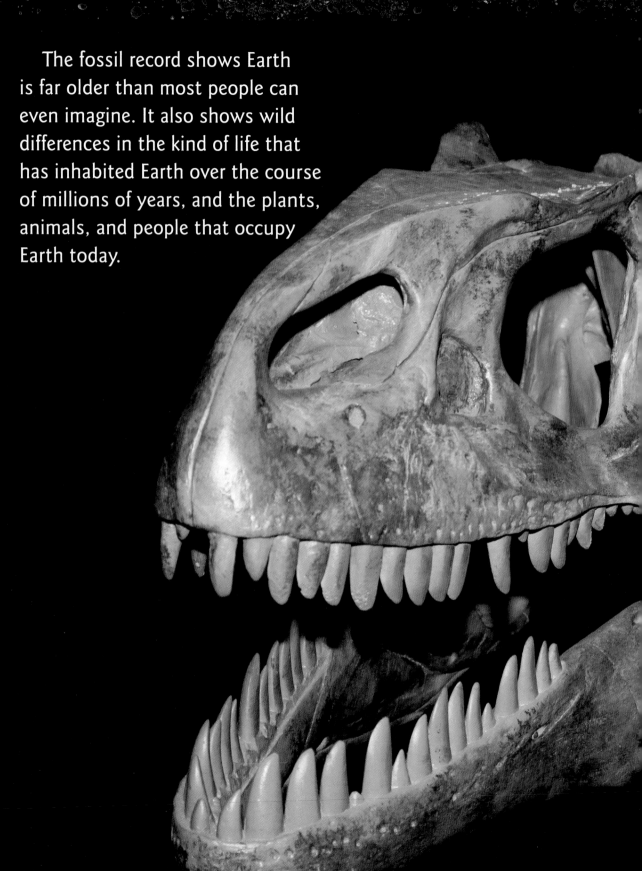

The fossil record shows Earth is far older than most people can even imagine. It also shows wild differences in the kind of life that has inhabited Earth over the course of millions of years, and the plants, animals, and people that occupy Earth today.

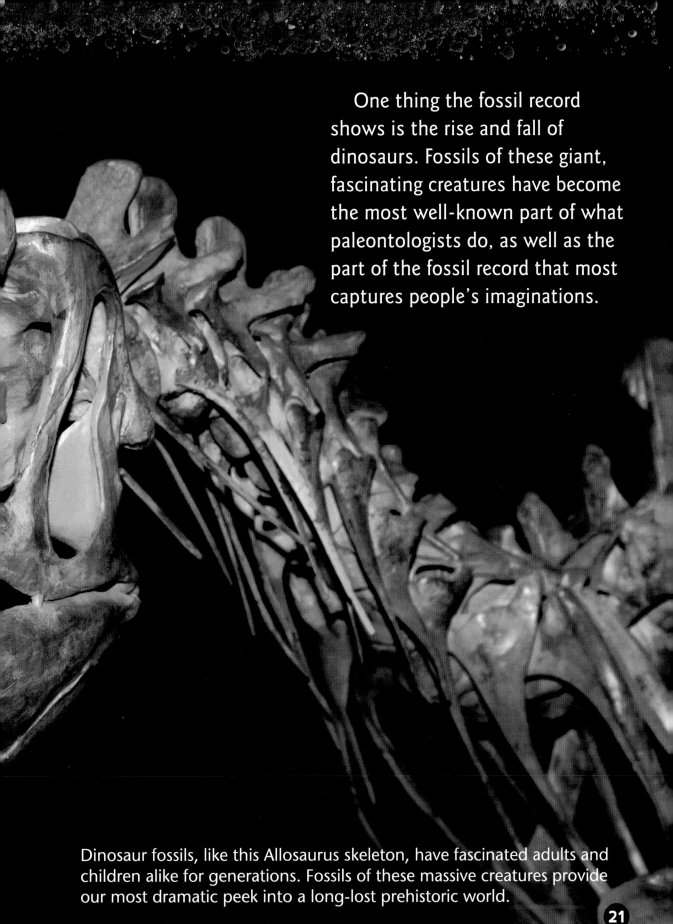

One thing the fossil record shows is the rise and fall of dinosaurs. Fossils of these giant, fascinating creatures have become the most well-known part of what paleontologists do, as well as the part of the fossil record that most captures people's imaginations.

Dinosaur fossils, like this Allosaurus skeleton, have fascinated adults and children alike for generations. Fossils of these massive creatures provide our most dramatic peek into a long-lost prehistoric world.

In some areas on Earth, layers of sedimentary rock are known to be of a certain age and therefore, more likely to hold certain types of fossils left by animals from that time.

The term Jurassic refers to a specific time in prehistory when, according to fossil evidence, dinosaurs roamed the Earth.

GEOLOGIC TIME AND THE

Precambrian, or early Earth, era:
from 4.5 billion years ago until 570 million years ago. Very few fossils, mostly simple life forms like algae and small worms.

Paleozoic, or ancient life, era:
from 570 million years ago until 245 million years ago. Fossils range from small creatures with no backbone to earliest signs of amphibians crawling onto land.

Mesozoic, or middle life, era:
from 245 million years ago until 65 million years ago. Fossils show the rise and extinction of dinosaurs through the Cretaceous, Jurassic, and Triassic epochs.

Cenozoic, or recent life, era:
from 65 million years ago to present. Fossils show the rise of mammals, including early horses, apes, mammoths, and the rise of humans.

Paleontologists place fossils in the geologic timeline of Earth. The fossil record includes four main eras of time representing about 4.5 billion years of Earth's geologic history.

Each **era** includes **epochs** representing millions of years of fossil history and the rock strata in which paleontologists found those fossils.

FOSSIL RECORD IN BRIEF

DIGGING UP THE PAST

Nothing adds to the fossil record until a person finds a **specimen** and studies it. Paleontologists work hard to understand a particular group of plants or animals, and the strata that would most likely hold their fossils, before they try to dig them up and study them. This is one area where geology and paleontology are so closely related.

Some places, such as the Burgess Shale in western Canada, are hotbeds of fossil discoveries. For more than 100 years, paleontologists have flocked here to find fossils of small, soft-bodied, prehistoric animals buried in the rocks at the site.

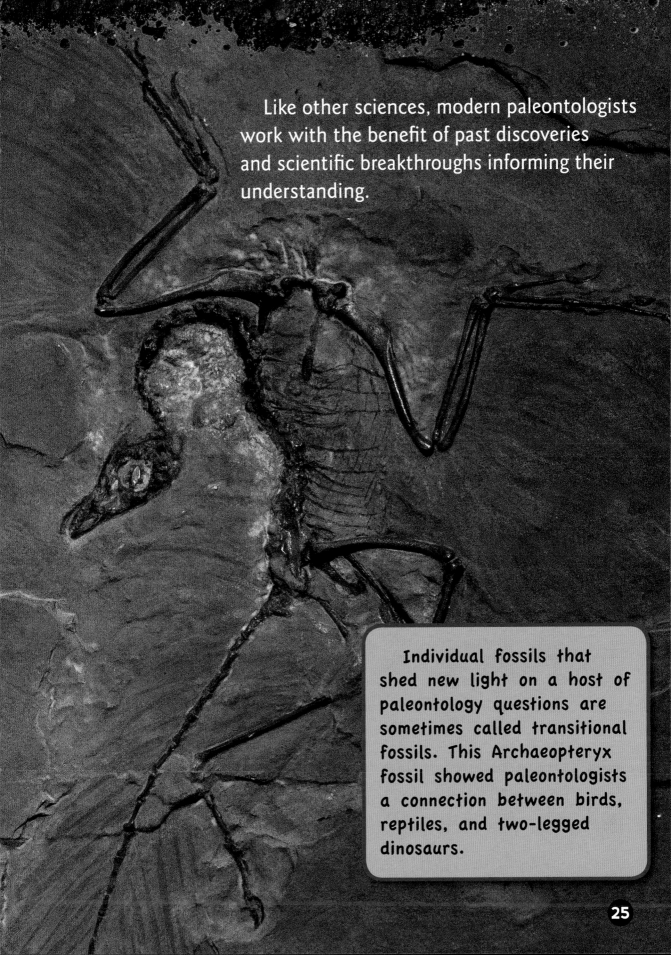

Like other sciences, modern paleontologists work with the benefit of past discoveries and scientific breakthroughs informing their understanding.

Individual fossils that shed new light on a host of paleontology questions are sometimes called transitional fossils. This Archaeopteryx fossil showed paleontologists a connection between birds, reptiles, and two-legged dinosaurs.

Knowing the age of fossils is trickier than knowing the age of trees. If a tree is cut down, a cross-cut section of the trunk reveals rings. Each ring represents about one year of life. In 1964, a massive Bristlecone pine tree cut down in Nevada had 4,900 rings. The tree, nicknamed Prometheus, is the oldest known tree on Earth.

FIELD NOTES

A paleontologist reads the age of a fossil specimen by using a complex scientific process known as **radiometric** dating. Similar to the rings of a tree trunk providing a built-in clock or calendar to mark a tree's age, fossils contain measurable **radioactivity** that mark their rate of decay. This decay rate is constant for different elements found in rocks and can provide an accurate measurement of a specimen's age.

HAVE CLOCKS

THE CHEMISTRY AND MATH OF HALF-LIFE MEASUREMENTS

As long as a plant or animal is living, the amount of carbon it contains remains constant. However, once it dies, the amount of carbon begins to decrease. The amount of time it takes for half of the carbon atoms of something to decay is its **half-life**. In the case of carbon, its half-life is 5,730 years. That means every 5,730 years, the carbon in a specimen will be reduced by half again. By measuring carbon or other decay isotopes in some fossils, paleontologists can measure how many half-lives have passed since the fossilized animal or plant died.

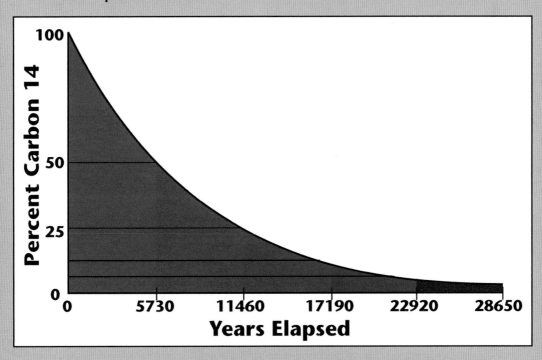

Not every working paleontologist spends all of his or her time digging in rocks in remote places. Many paleontologists teach. Some write about things other scientists have found, or hope to find. For those who do field research looking for fossils, there is much work to do before ever heading out with their digging tools.

Working in the field means bringing many tools to a dig site. Paleontologists use digital computer technology such as global positioning systems (GPS) to document exact locations in addition to more traditional tools for breaking, cutting or shaving rocks.

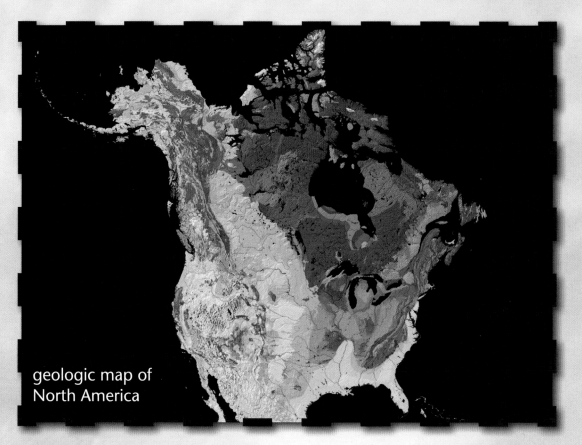

geologic map of
North America

Geologic maps help researchers identify certain strata that are more likely to hold fossils of a certain type. Since sedimentary rock is the most effective at preserving fossils, paleontologists study areas to find spots where ancient lakes, rivers, or other water sources might have aided in fossil creation.

Paleontologists find fossils in the strangest places. Fossil finds in what is now the state of Kentucky include many prehistoric animals that lived in the sea. This discovery led paleontologists to theorize that some dry land areas on Earth, such as Kentucky, may have once been under water.

Field research is not cheap. A fossil hunting expedition takes time, tools, planning, and people to be successful. This means before paleontologists head out to dig for fossils, they need to secure **funding** to help pay for their work, supplies, transportation, and support.

DIGGING TAKES DOLLARS

Paleontologists write proposals for research projects to get funding from a university, museum, or the National Science Foundation, which is set up by the United States government to help advance scientific knowledge. The NSF is involved in all areas of scientific study, so the percentage of paleontology research funded by the group is relatively small. In some cases, paleontologists will pay for their own research and rely on volunteer science enthusiasts to help with the project.

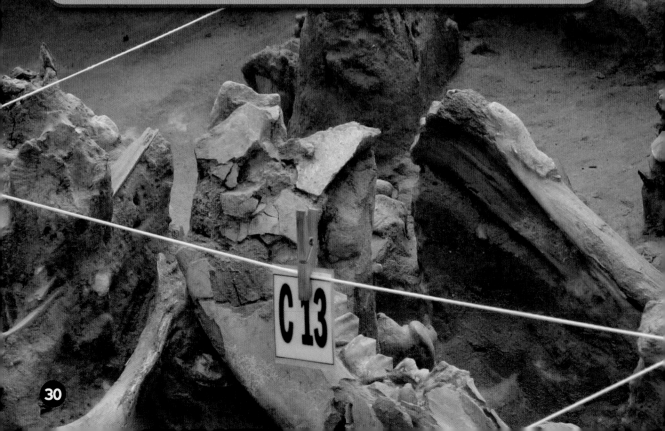

Research paleontologists have to come prepared. Often, the hunt for fossils takes place in remote areas, far from the comforts of home or even civilization. Once a paleontologist finds a specimen, documents the location and strata, special care goes into removing the fossil from the ground and protecting it from damage until it is brought to a lab for dating and study.

Paleontologists digging for fossils create a grid of string or rope over their dig site. The marked grid helps them keep a detailed track of where each specimen was found.

Paleontologists, like baseball players, don't like to strike out in their hunt for fossil specimens. Knowing where to look, using previous scientific discoveries about certain fossilized species and the characteristics of the rock strata where they were previously discovered, can lead to what some might call a higher paleo-batting average.

Many paleontologists enjoy field research because it allows them to work outside, doing what they enjoy, surrounded by natural beauty.

Physically walking around an area to scout specific research locations also helps the success rate of a research project and drives up the paleo-batting average. This is especially true when rock strata is very close to the ground's surface or is even exposed. Researchers call these exposed layers outcrops.

SENSATIONAL SCIENTIST

Sue Hendrickson is an amateur dinosaur bone hunter. She was assisting on a paleontology research project in the South Dakota Badlands in 1990 when she took a short hike and found what appeared to be three huge fossilized bones exposed in a remote outcrop. Her keen eyes had found the most complete Tyrannosaurus Rex skeleton ever discovered. The fearsome fossil, nicknamed Sue, remains on permanent display at Chicago's Field Museum of Natural History. In addition to paleontology research, Sue is an expert scuba diver and explorer.

PALEONTOLOGY: A RHYME OF GEOLOGIC TIME

The Earth is far older than the human race
Fossils show life coming and going at a snail's pace

So much of what lived before history began
Lies buried in rock layers beneath the land

There are fascinating changes throughout life's history
Paleontologists work to solve the scientific mystery

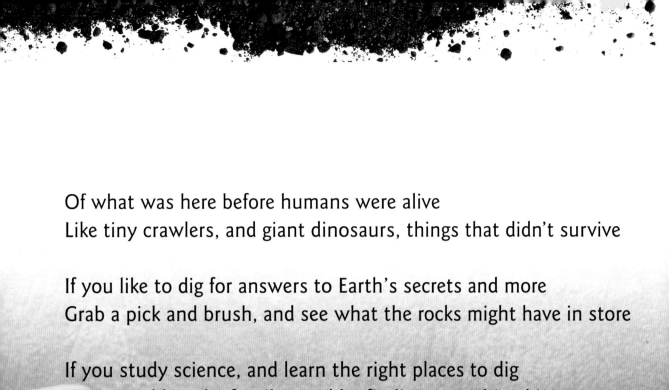

Of what was here before humans were alive
Like tiny crawlers, and giant dinosaurs, things that didn't survive

If you like to dig for answers to Earth's secrets and more
Grab a pick and brush, and see what the rocks might have in store

If you study science, and learn the right places to dig
You can add to the fossil record by finding something big!

Paleontology, like other areas of scientific study, offers young people many opportunities to get involved.

Citizen scientist programs promote amateur participation in actual research projects, including fossil hunts.

FIELD NOTES

The study of fossils left by plants is called paleobotany. Plant fossils provide clues about climate, soil, and other parts of prehistoric Earth.

At Oregon's John Day Fossil Beds National Park, paleontologists have found a treasure trove of Cenozoic age fossils. The fossil beds contain many specimens of extinct mammals, all dating back less than 50 million years. That's an immense amount of human time, but a relatively small chunk of geologic time.

Paleontologists have to be multi-faceted scientists. A single research project can involve elements of chemistry, geology, physics, and other disciplines, sometimes all in the same day.

Many universities and museums perform research projects that depend on citizen scientists to perform at least some of the field work.

THE MASTODON MATRIX PROJECT

Like woolly mammoths, prehistoric mastodons resembled elephants. This complete mastodon skeleton was found in 1845 and is on display at New York City's American Museum of Natural History.

Thousands of students have helped analyze pieces of sediment found around the bones from a real mastodon dig. The project is a large-scale collaboration between a museum and hundreds of volunteer student groups. The open-ended, educational project relies on students to dig through chunks of dirt and rock looking for fossil fragments or other clues left behind by the extinct elephant-like **Ice Age** creatures.

Based on fossil evidence, modern reconstructions of mastodons show them to have low shoulders and massive tusks. They roamed forested areas of what is now the United States. Thomas Jefferson, one of the United States' founding fathers and third president, kept a collection of mastodon bones.

The Ice Age refers to a time when the polar ice caps grew and covered large parts of the continents. In geologic time, the last great ice age was just a short time ago. Fossils of mastodons and other mammals date to as recent as 10,000 years ago. Today, paleontologists and other scientists are studying the possibilities of another catastrophic climate change affecting life on Earth.

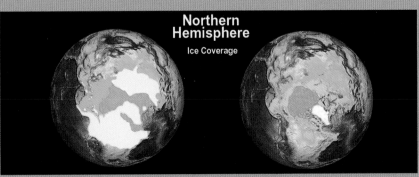

Northern Hemisphere
Ice Coverage

18,000 years ago   **Modern Day**

☐ Continental ice   ☐ Sea ice   ☐ Land above sea level

Note: Modern sea ice coverage represents summer months

If you like exploring and adventure, and if you like the idea of discovering artifacts so old they predate the reach of human history, you might want to pursue becoming a citizen scientist in paleontology research.

Over the years, paleontologists' discovery of dinosaur bones and other fossils have been the basis of many popular books, TV shows, and movies. These, in turn, inspire more people to consider careers in paleontology.

Signs of Earth's past are all around us. Take note as you encounter nature. Do you see rocky outcrops? If you take a ride along a highway through mountainous terrain, do you see rock layers plainly visible wherever a hillside has been cut away to make room for the highway? Those layers are the stuff of paleontology.

WAYS TO GET INVOLVED

Besides taking science classes in school, young people interested in paleontology can find research opportunities at local museums and universities, or by searching online. It's a great way to turn interest into action.

SHARK!

Programs such as PaleoQuest.org's Sharkfinder program let young science enthusiasts assist professional researchers in hunting for shark and stingray fossils in coastal sediment along the edge of the Chesapeake Bay in Maryland and Virginia. Their discoveries can add to the fossil record and some specimens even end up on display at a museum.

TIMELINE

Pre-1500
Fossilized bones generally thought to be either the work of demons, or the remains of mythical dragons.

1600s
Scientists first note similarity between the shape of shark's teeth and fossils called tongue stones. First scientific theories emerge explaining the stones could have once been teeth of living creatures.

1664
Danish scholar Nicolaus Steno theorizes rock layers get deposited over time with older layers below more recent layers.

Nicolaus Steno
1638-1686

1796
Cuvier's theory of extinct species explains fossil oddities.

1858
Nearly complete dinosaur skeleton fossil discovered in New Jersey. The specimen was named Hadrosaurus.

1859
Darwin publishes *On the Origin of Species*, his scientific theory of evolution through natural selection.

By 1868, the Hadrosaurus fossil became the first dinosaur fossil mounted for public view, at Philadelphia's Academy of Natural Sciences.

1861
Archaeopteryx "bird-lizard" fossil discovered in Germany.

Othniel Charles Marsh
1831-1899

Edward Cope
1840-1897

1870s
"Dinosaur Wars" - Early American paleontologists O.C. March and Edward Cope make a series of competing fossil discoveries across the American West.

1902
First T-Rex fossil discovered, goes on display at New York's American Museum of Natural History.

1960s
Paleontology enters pop-culture with popular cartoon *The Flintstones*. The fictional stone-age family has a pet dinosaur.

1990
Nearly 90 percent complete Tyrannosaurus fossil, nicknamed Sue, discovered in South Dakota.

1993
Blockbuster film *Jurassic Park* amazes audiences worldwide with life-like depictions of various dinosaurs and their behaviors.

Present day
Fossils of long-extinct life forms from prehistoric plants to dinosaurs continue thrilling visitors at natural history museums worldwide.

Glossary

biology (bi-AH-luh-jee): scientific study of living things

catastrophic (kuh-TASS-truh-fik): having to do with natural disasters

chemistry (KEH-miss-tree): scientific study of the structure and makeup of things

epochs (E-poks): time periods within specific eras

era (E-ruh): long periods of time that include multiple epochs

fossils (FAH-suhlz): preserved remains from previous geologic ages

funding (FUN-ding): a source of money used to pay for a project

half-life (HAF-life): time required to lose half of an object's radioactivity

Ice Age (EYSS-ayj): prehistoric time when polar ice covered land

physics (FIZ-ehks): scientific study of matter and energy

prehistoric (pree-hiz-TOH-rik): something that pre-dates humans

radioactivity (ray-dee-o-ak-TIV-eh-tee): decay-related emission of energetic particles

radiometric (ray-dee-o-MEH-trik): means of measuring decay rates

sediment (SEH-duh-muhnt): mud which turns into layers of rock

specimen (SPEH-sih-mehn): a physical sample

strata (STRA-tuh): fossil-bearing sedimentary rock

Index

Show What You Know

1. What is the scientific name of rock layers where fossils are buried?

2. What important biological occurrence did George Cuvier first propose to be true?

3. What needs to happen to an animal's remains fairly quickly for it to become fossilized?

4. What did Sue Hendrickson find?

5. What process do paleontologists use to determine the age of a fossil?

Websites to Visit

www.paleoportal.org

www.museumoftheearth.org

www.paleoquest.org

About the Author

Tom Greve lives in Chicago with his wife and two kids. He has always been fascinated by dinosaurs and the mysteries of prehistoric times. He enjoys visiting Sue the T-Rex at Chicago's Field Museum.

Meet The Author!
www.meetREMauthors.com

PHOTO CREDITS: Cover: Bottom photo © Salajean | Dreamstime.com, dinosaur skeleton © Rod Beverley / shutterstock; header photo of dirt © Madlen; page 4-5 © MarcelClemens; page 6-7: rocky landscape © Alexander Tihonov, sandy beach © Linda Brotkorb, snowy maountains © Alita Bobrov, rocky beach © elxeneize, geologist © welzevoul; page 9 © Natursports; page 10 © prudkov, page 11 © Kenneth Keifer; page 12-13 © Kenneth Sponsler, page 12 bottom right © Anton_Ivanov, bottom left © EcoPrint; page 14 left © Teguh Mujiono, right © thomas koch, page 15 left © stockphoto mania, right © Igor Karasi; page 16 © Nils Knötschke wikimedia, page 17 top left © AlessandroZocc, top right © Ivan Smuk, bottom left © 24Novembers, bottom right © BGSmith; page 19 mammoth bones © Goran Bogicevic; page 20-21 © Steve Bower; page 23 top © Inc, page 25 © Wlad74; page 26 courtesy of Arpingstone, page 28 inset © Rich Koele, page 28-29 © shutterstock Image ID: 126195974, page 29 map courtesy of USGS; page 31 © Duard van der Westhuizen; page 32 © Natursports, page 33 © Dallas Krentzel; page 34-35 © Styve Reineck; page 36 © APaterson, page 37 © Anatoliy Lukich, inset photo courtesy of National Park Service; page 38 © Ryan Somma, page 39 © Dantheman9758 at the English language Wikipedia, globes courtesy of NOAA; page 40-41 © Linda Bucklin; page 42 © Jonathan Lenz, page 43 © Ivan Smuk; page 44 © Jim, the Photographer from Springfield PA

Edited by: Keli Sipperley

Cover and Interior design by: Nicola Stratford   www.nicolastratford.com

Library of Congress PCN Data

Paleontologists / Tom Greve
(Scientists in the Field)
ISBN 978-1-63430-411-5 (hard cover)
ISBN 978-1-63430-511-2 (soft cover)
ISBN 978-1-63430-603-4(e-Book)
Library of Congress Control Number: 2015931712

Also Available as:

Printed in the United States of America, North Mankato, Minnesota